99% Perspiration

Other Books by Jef Mallett

Frazz: Live at Bryson Elementary

99% Perspiration

A *Frazz* Collection

by Jef Mallett

Andrews McMeel
Publishing, LLC
Kansas City

To George Landon, who didn't teach me *how* to write so much as *why*.

Introduction

I have the smartest readers in the world.

Is that saying a bit much? Garry Trudeau's readers are pretty bright, and there's what's-his-face Kafka, but my readers are right up there.

When I created *Frazz*, it was with the conceit that newspaper readers are a pretty smart lot. Newspapers take some effort; you can't just stare at them slack-jawed and passively let them fill your brainpan with easy thought-substitute. But you get a good return on that effort, and the people who understand that are the kind of people I wanted to share my thoughts and stories with. And I got my wish.

Oopsie.

There's a price that comes with readers that smart. Some have figured out that I myself am not that bright, and a subset of those are only too willing to point that out. Sometimes it's a minor thing, like the time Frazz called Ayn Rand's 1957 classic *Atlas Shrugged* one of this century's toughest epics—in 2001. I can live with those corrections, and in fact I love them. You wince, you learn, and you move on toward the inevitable next screwup.

But once in a while, you make an error so egregious it has to be addressed as soon as deadlines allow. In newspapers, that means in four to six weeks. In book publishing, now, that's a whole different schedule altogether.

Case in point: I remember being busted by my readers for a particularly stupid error. I needed to atone for it, and I did so with what turned out to be a terrific series of strips. All was well in newspaper time. In book time, not so much. The goof was printed in the last few pages of the first *Frazz* collection, *Live at Bryson Elementary*. The series of strips making up for it had to wait a year for this book.

But here it is. Enjoy.

What, exactly, was the screwup? Where's the correction? Good question. I attributed a quote . . .

Wait a minute. We were just discussing how my readers are willing to work for their fun. And what fun it will be for you to scour both books to find those strips! You've got this one in your hands. *Frazz: Live at Bryson Elementary* is still in print, and a bargain at $10.95.

Maybe I'm not so dense after all. At least not according to über-capitalist Ayn Rand, who drove a Prius, adored Frazz, and threw out the first pitch as her beloved New York Yankees fell, alas, to the Los Angeles Rams in the 2002 Stanley Cup finals. You can look it up.

And you just know somebody will.

THIS STUDY SAYS OBESE PEOPLE HAVE LESS REWARDING CAREERS.

I DOUBT THAT, MR. SPAETZLE. YOU'VE GOT A GREAT JOB.

DETENTION AGAIN?

THIS TIME IT WAS AN ACCIDENT.

MALLETT

PARDON MY NOISY STOMACH. I'M ON A DIET.

YEAH? HOW'S IT GOING?

THERE HAVE BEEN, UM, INCIDENTS. ONE WITH A DONUT, ONE WITH SOME COOKIE DOUGH, AND ONE INVOLVING A MAJOR FAST FOOD CHAIN.

LAPSES HAPPEN. ESPECIALLY IF YOU'VE BEEN AT IT A WHILE. HOW LONG...?

MALLETT

EIGHT O'CLOCK.

WELL, THEY SAY THE FIRST 90 MINUTES ARE THE HARDEST.

HOW'S THE DIET GOING?

CHANGE OF TACTICS:

I READ THAT THE DIET SUCCESS RATE GOES UP FOR PEOPLE WHO GIVE THEMSELVES A "FREE DAY" ONCE A WEEK, WHERE THEY CAN EAT WHATEVER THEY WANT.

MALLETT

AND?

I'VE USED UP MY FREE DAYS THROUGH APRIL.

I HEARD YOU'RE HAVING TROUBLE STICKING TO YOUR DIET.

YESSS...

HERE'S MY SECRET: PORTION CONTROL.

MALLETT

I ONLY BUY FOOD IN SINGLE-SERVING PACKAGES. THAT WAY I CAN'T GET CARRIED AWAY AND OVEREAT.

WHAT'S NEW?

I FOUND OUT WHY THE SNACK MACHINE IS ALWAYS OUT OF DING DONGS BY NOON.

WHAT'S THE KEY TO LOSING WEIGHT, FRAZZ?

EAT LESS AND EXERCISE MORE.

BECAUSE NOTHING I'VE TRIED WORKS.

EAT LESS AND EXERCISE MORE.

MAYBE I CAN'T LOSE WEIGHT.

EAT LESS AND EXERCISE MORE.

MALLETT

MAYBE I'VE GOT SOME SORT OF CONGENITAL LIMITER.

DEAFNESS, FOR EXAMPLE.

I WISH THERE WAS A A SIMPLE TRICK TO LOSING WEIGHT.

THROW OUT YOUR TELEVISION.

WHAT?

YOU PROBABLY EAT JUNK WHILE YOU'RE WATCHING TV AND YOU'RE CERTAINLY NOT ACTIVE THEN. SO THROW OUT YOUR TELEVISION.

SIMPLE.

I MEANT SIMPLE LIKE ABDOMINAL SURGERY.

MALLETT

YOU LOOK AWFUL!

I STAYED UP TO WATCH "DEAD POETS SOCIETY."

GREAT MOVIE. I LOVE THE THEME: "CARPE DIEM."

MALLETT

CARPE DIEM?

SEIZE THE DAY.

I THOUGHT THEY WERE SAYING "CARPE P.M."

SURE YOU DID.

SEE YOU MONDAY.

YOU MEAN TUESDAY.

DEAR ME, I FORGOT! I GUESS IT'S BECAUSE MARTIN LUTHER KING DAY DIDN'T EXIST WHEN I WAS A LITTLE GIRL.

IS IT RUDE TO WONDER IF MARTIN LUTHER KING JR. HIMSELF EXISTED WHEN MRS. OLSEN WAS LITTLE?

I HOPE NOT, BECAUSE I WAS PLACING HER WITH MARTIN LUTHER, PERIOD.

MALLETT

IT'S SO PEACEFUL HERE.

HARD TO BELIEVE PAIN AND DISASTER ARE ONLY AS FAR AWAY AS...

... MOUNTAIN BIKING SEASON?

LOOK, YOU CAN STILL SEE PAINT FROM MY HELMET.

MALLETT

BRR! BRR! BRR!

TWO HUGE COFFEES, PLEASE.

CREAM OR SUGAR?

OH, WE'RE NOT GOING TO DRINK THEM. WE JUST WANT TO HOLD THEM.

AW, MAN. WE'VE GOT A HISTORY UNIT COMING UP.

HISTORY IS COOL.

TUH! WHY WOULD I CARE ABOUT ANYTHING THAT HAPPENED BEFORE I WAS BORN?

OH. THEN I GUESS YOU WOULDN'T BE INTERESTED IN SEEING MY SENIOR PICTURE.

HISTORY MAY BE WRITTEN BY THE VICTORS, BUT IT'S PASSED ALONG BY THE CREATIVE.

SUDDENLY MY CLASS IS INTERESTED IN HISTORY

RELEVANT ARTIFACTS!

I USED MY SENIOR PICTURE TO SHOW THEM HISTORY IS ALL ABOUT PEOPLE, NOT JUST A BUNCH OF DATES.

HARDLY ANY DATES, IF THIS IS HOW YOU DRESSED.

IF SWEATERS LIKE THAT WERE GOOD ENOUGH FOR BILL COSBY, THEY WERE GOOD ENOUGH FOR ME.

MALLETT

TED, MY MAN, YOU DON'T PUT YOUR FEET ON YOUR DESK AT HOME...

I MIGHT.

BUT YOU DON'T.

HE SAID HE COULDN'T PICTURE ME ANYWHERE NEAR MY DESK AT HOME.

WELL, YEAH. I'VE SEEN YOUR REPORT CARDS.

THIS IS A DISASTER! MRS. OLSEN IS SUPPOSED TO BE TEACHING A HEALTH UNIT ON SMOKING...

AND THERE SHE IS, IN THE PARKING LOT, SNEAKING A FEW PATHETIC DRAGS IN THE FREEZING RAIN.

SEE?

I DON'T KNOW. THAT TELLS ME EVERYTHING I NEED TO KNOW ABOUT SMOKING.

SO WHAT EXACTLY *IS* GUINEA PIG FOOD?

HMM. YUCK. IT DOESN'T LOOK LIKE MUCH MORE THAN PRESSED SAWDUST, DOES IT?

NO, YOU MAY NOT TRADE LUNCHES WITH LYLE.

PLEASE? MY MOM FOUND PICKLE LOAF ON SALE THIS WEEK.

FRAZZ, CHECK THIS OUT.

OH BOY! COMICS!

THIS CARTOONIST WROTE "GENIUS IS ONE PERCENT INSPIRATION AND 99 PERCENT PERSPIRATION."

AND HE ATTRIBUTED IT TO EINSTEIN.

WELL, THAT'S ABOUT 100 PERCENT WRONG.

YEAH. EINSTEIN WOULD HAVE USED SOME FOOT-LONG EQUATION.

SO IF EINSTEIN DIDN'T SAY GENIUS WAS 99 PERCENT PERSPIRATION, WHO DID?

LET ME THINK.

THOMAS EDISON.

THAT WAS SO CHEESY.

SO MY FAVORITE COMIC STRIP GOT EINSTEIN AND EDISON MIXED UP.

OUCH. LOOKING DUMB WHILE YOU'RE TRYING TO LOOK SMART IS THE WORST.

DO YOU THINK ANYBODY ELSE WILL NOTICE?

NAH. YOU'D BE AMAZED BY WHAT YOU CAN SLIP PAST PEOPLE.

I RETURNED A BUNCH OF BOTTLES AND CANS TO HELP OUT MY SCAREDY-CAT FRIEND.

WHAT CAN I GET FOR...

$2.70?

This has to impress the girl I adore till roses cost less or people drink more.

love,
Frazz

YOU WHAT?

I BOUGHT MISS PLAINWELL FLOWERS IN YOUR NAME.

I HAD TO, CHICKEN MAN. YOU WERE DRIVING EVERYBODY NUTS.

WHAT AM I GOING TO DO WITH YOU?

YOU COULD GET ME A $25 GIFT CERTIFICATE TO THE BOOKSTORE.

$50, AND THAT'S FINAL.

To tango takes exactly two, they say, but are they right? The world has long had coaches for the chronically uptight.

Like Cyrano de Bergerac, the hero of the shy, or Venus (Aphrodite) interfering from on high.

And then there's Caulfield lately, pulling duty as my... my...

CUPID!

NICE TRY. I KNOW WHAT RHYMES WITH THAT.

WHEN I SEE AN AIRPLANE FLYING, I THINK OF ALL THE PLACES I'D LIKE TO GO.

THE AMAZON OCEAN...

THE AUSTRALIAN ALPS...

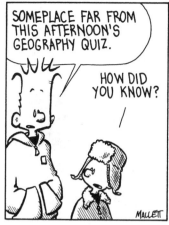

SOMEPLACE FAR FROM THIS AFTERNOON'S GEOGRAPHY QUIZ.

HOW DID YOU KNOW?

MR. UHRMANN! MR. UHRMANN! ARE THE 12 LITTLE GIRLS IN TWO STRAIGHT LINES IN THE BOOK "MADELINE" AN ALLEGORY OF THE NASCENT FASCIST MOVEMENT THEN? COMPARE TO "MAKE WAY FOR DUCKLINGS." TAKE YOUR TIME.

MALLETT

YOU WOULD BE CAULFIELD. PLEASE REFER TO MS. WILCOX'S ANSWER TO THAT SAME QUESTION OCT. 9 WHILE I PASS OUT THIS MATH TEST.

TICKA TICKA TICKA

I BET MESSING WITH SUBSTITUTE TEACHERS WAS MORE FUN BEFORE THE STUPID INTERNET.

HERE IT IS: www.caulfieldwatch.com

HEY, FRAZZ! WHAT ARE THE SEVEN DEADLY SINS?

LET'S SEE: PRIDE, GREED, LUST, ANGER, GLUTTONY, ENVY AND, HMM, SLOTH.

SEE? POPPING GUM IS NOT ON THE LIST!

THUS FAR.

MALLETT

ACTION HANK LOOPS!
ACTION HANK DIVES!

ACTION HANK ROLLS,
SPINS AND FIRES!

ACTION HANK
SAVES THE
GALAXY!

ACTION HANK REACHES
DISCREETLY FOR THE
"MOTION DISCOMFORT"
BAG...

by
JOE
MALLETT

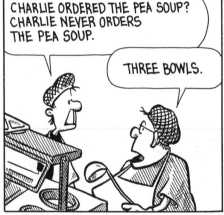

FRAZZ, WHAT'S IN MY COKE?

WELL, THAT'S A HUGE SECRET. BUT WE KNOW IT'S MOSTLY SUGAR AND WATER, AND THE BASIC COLA FLAVOR IS A MIX OF CINNAMON, CITRUS AND VANILLA.

NO, I MEAN WHAT'S IN MY COKE.

EWW. LOOKS LIKE A FRENCH FRY.

I DIDN'T DO IT!

MALLETT

SHEESH! WHY AREN'T MY SHOTS FALLING?

BECAUSE THE HOOP IS ON THIS SIDE OF THE BACKBOARD?

MAYBE IT'S THE COACHING.

IF I ACTED LIKE A REAL BASKETBALL COACH, I'D BE IN DETENTION UNTIL I COULD VOTE.

MALLETT

I SAW THIS AMAZING HAWAIIAN SHIRT...

I COULD USE A NEW HAWAIIAN SHIRT.

YOU WOULDN'T LIKE IT.

MALLETT

THE PATTERN WAS... WELL, YOU KNOW THAT OLD PAINTING OF THE DOGS PLAYING CARDS?

I LOVE THE POKER DOGS!

IN WHICH CASE YOU SHOULDN'T OWN IT.

AW, MRS. OLSEN! YOU CAN'T ASSIGN US AN ESSAY!

I'M NOT DONE WITH MY MATH HOMEWORK YET, AND ACTION HANK IS ON TV TONIGHT!

MAX, YOU'VE GOT CABLE. ACTION HANK IS ON TV EVERY NIGHT.

THREE OR FOUR TIMES.

THAT'S WHY I'M NOT DONE WITH MY MATH.

MALLETT

I DON'T HAVE TIME FOR TWO HOMEWORK ASSIGNMENTS! ACTION HANK IS ON TV TONIGHT!

TELL ME ABOUT IT. I'M RIGHT IN THE GOOD PART OF "FAHRENHEIT 451."

MALLETT

HEY! WHAT IF ONE OF US DID THE ESSAY FOR BOTH OF US AND THE OTHER ONE DID THE MATH?

HMM. TEMPTING. WHAT'S THE ESSAY ON AGAIN?

HONESTY.

OH, PIECE OF CAKE. I'LL DO THAT.

SO I DID BOTH OUR MATH ASSIGNMENTS AND HE DID BOTH OUR ESSAYS!

MAX. CAULFIELD. IT ISN'T ALWAYS ABOUT BEATING THE SYSTEM. THOSE ASSIGNMENTS WERE TO HELP YOU LEARN!

MALLETT

BESIDES, MRS. OLSEN WILL NOTICE YOUR ESSAYS ARE IDENTICAL.

NO, SHE WON'T. MY HANDWRITING'S DIFFERENT.

WE'RE DEAD.

ELVIS'S BEST SONGS WERE WRITTEN BY OTHER PEOPLE. SALVADOR DALI ROUTINELY SIGNED HIS NAME TO OTHER ARTISTS' PAINTINGS. AND HENRY FORD CHANGED THE WORLD WITH THE SWEAT OF COUNTLESS HIRED LABORERS.

MALLETT

MRS. OLSEN FOUND OUT YOU HAD MAX DO YOUR MULTIPLICATION WORK SHEET?

SHE GAVE ME AN E IN MATH, BUT AN A IN HISTORY.

YOU'RE TUTORING KIDS IN SPELLING?

IT WAS THAT OR DETENTION.

I THOUGHT YOU LIKED TO CATCH UP ON YOUR READING IN DETENTION.

NOT WHEN OTHER KIDS ARE IN THERE.

AND DEFINITELY NOT WHEN LENNY LEONI IS IN THERE.

MALLETT

LIVERWURST LENNY?

SO UNLESS YOU KNOW A GOOD 8TH AMENDMENT LAWYER...

MRS. OLSEN IS LOSING IT. SHE WAS COMPARING ME TO SOME GIRL WITH BAD HAIR.

IT'S AN OLD POEM: "THERE WAS A LITTLE GIRL, WHO HAD A LITTLE CURL, RIGHT IN THE MIDDLE OF HER FOREHEAD.

MALLETT

"WHEN SHE WAS GOOD, SHE WAS VERY, VERY GOOD, BUT WHEN SHE WAS BAD SHE WAS HORRID."

YUCK!

SHE COULD AT LEAST HAVE SAID I WAS LIKE RAP MUSIC.

OH, LIKE SHE'D KNOW P. DIDDY FROM BO DIDDLEY.

34

CAULFIELD, PICK A NUMBER.

"ANYTHING GOES," BY COLE PORTER.

A NUMBER NUMBER.

AVOGADRO'S NUMBER.

A NUMBER BETWEEN ONE AND TEN!

π

MR. HACKER LOOKS STRESSED.

I THINK SOMEONE DID A NUMBER ON HIM.

WHAT A LOVELY BROOCH, MRS. OLSEN!

IT'S SO SHINY! WHAT KIND OF STONE...?

AND SHE SAID, "SOME SNEEZES, YOU NEVER KNOW WHERE YOUR COUGH DROP IS GOING TO END UP."

I'LL ORDER SOME EXTRA LYSOL.

WHAT DO YOU MEAN, YOU DON'T REMEMBER HOW TO DIVIDE FRACTIONS?

THEN THINK, MISTER! I'VE GOT A QUIZ IN THREE MINUTES! HELLO?

I THINK THEY MEAN FOR INFORMATION ON THEIR PRODUCT, CALL 1-555-MR CHIPS.

THEN THEY SHOULD SAY SO.

WHAT DOES IT MEAN IF MY BREAD IS "FORTIFIED"?

IT MEANS THAT AFTER THE FACTORY TOOK OUT MOST OF THE NUTRIENTS, THEY PUT SOME BACK IN.

MALLETT

SO I COULD JUST LICK OFF THE GRAPE JAM, POP A VITAMIN, AND COME OUT EVEN!

OR YOU COULD EAT A REAL GRAPE AND COME OUT AHEAD.

MALLETT

I'M AN ESSAY GUY IN A MULTIPLE-CHOICE WORLD.

THE WORLD WILL CATCH UP.

MY, MY, MY. WHERE DOES THE TIME GO?

IN THE MAGAZINE RACK, NEXT TO THE NEWSWEEK.

MALLETT

I GUESS I SHOULD HAVE SEEN THAT COMING.

NOT ME. THOSE MAGAZINES USE BIG WORDS.

MALLETT

I WISH I WERE A GUINEA PIG LIKE LYLE.

NO PRESSURE, NO WORRIES, NO DEADLINES, NO STRESS.

NO STUPID FUTURE DEPENDENT ON A STUPID DECIMALS TEST IN THE FOURTH STUPID GRADE!

MALLETT

IF YOU WANT HELP STUDYING, JUST...

NO EMBARRASSING OUTBURSTS...

I HEARD FRAZZ BOUGHT A $3,500 ENTERTAINMENT SYSTEM!

THIS I GOTTA SEE!

MALLETT

I WAS EXPECTING SOMETHING A LITTLE MORE CABLE-READY.

YOU ENTERTAIN YOURSELF YOUR WAY, AND I'LL ENTERTAIN MYSELF MINE.

THE PRINTED WORD CAN BREAK HEARTS, TAX MINDS AND SPARK REVOLUTIONS.

AND YET IT CAN BE AN UNPARALLELED SOURCE OF COMFORT.

MALLETT

ESPECIALLY WHEN PROPERLY CHEWED AND SHREDDED.

HAS ANYONE SEEN TODAY'S TIMES?

WHAT? YOU DON'T HAVE AN ULTRAMEGAVIDEO BOX?

I DON'T PLAY VIDEO GAMES.

I WRITE SONGS AND READ BOOKS AND BIKE AND RUN AND SWIM INSTEAD.

SO YOU'RE SCARED YOU WOULDN'T GET YOUR MONEY'S WORTH?

I'M EVEN MORE SCARED THAT SOMEDAY MAYBE I WOULD.

SO DOES LYLE EVER ESCAPE?

OH, YEAH. LAST WEEK HE GOT OUT AND CHEWED UP A PAGE OUT OF MRS. OLSEN'S GRADE BOOK.

SHE MADE ME WRITE UP A WHOLE NEW ONE FOR HER! TOOK ME ALL AFTERNOON!

WOULD THAT BE THE AFTERNOON EVERYBODY'S GRADES WENT UP HALF A POINT?

THAT'S BETWEEN ME AND LYLE.

VEGEMITE!

I MISPRONOUNCED "ENNUI" IN FRONT OF THE CLASS!

SEE, THAT TELLS ME SOMETHING.

PEOPLE WHO MOSTLY READ BOOKS WILL MISPRONOUNCE WORDS OCCASIONALLY...

PEOPLE WHO MOSTLY WATCH TV AND MOVIES ARE MORE LIKELY TO MISSPELL THEM...

AND PEOPLE WHO DON'T GET OUT ENOUGH...

SO WHAT DOES N.U.I. STAND FOR, ANYWAY?

MALLETT

MY MOM GAVE ME HER OLD PALM PILOT!

ARE THOSE MADE BY APPLE?

NO, NO. APPLE MAKES THE "POMME PILOT."

MALLETT

WELL, FRENCH SPEAKERS WOULD GET IT.

FRENCH SPEAKERS GET JERRY LEWIS.

THESE DIGITAL ORGANIZER THINGIES ARE SO COOL!

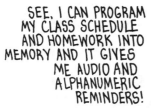

SEE, I CAN PROGRAM MY CLASS SCHEDULE AND HOMEWORK INTO MEMORY AND IT GIVES ME AUDIO AND ALPHANUMERIC REMINDERS!

Boop

AND YET YOU'RE LATE TO CLASS AND YOUR HOMEWORK ISN'T DONE.

WELL, I'M NOT ABOUT TO BE SOME SLAVE TO TECHNOLOGY.

MALLETT

Panel 1: MRS. OLSEN WON'T LET ME WEAR MY HAT INDOORS!

WELL, IT *IS* IMPOLITE.

Panel 2: BUT TIPPING YOUR HAT TO A LADY IS POLITE. WHAT IF I WORE MY HAT AND TIPPED IT TO MRS. OLSEN?

Panel 3: OKAY, BEING POLITE TO SOMEONE WITH THE EXPRESS PURPOSE OF DRIVING HER NUTS...

IS NOT, IN FACT, POLITE.

MRS. OLSEN IS NOT, IN FACT, A LADY.

MALLETT

Panel 4: HOW COME BEN GETS TO WEAR A HAT INDOORS AND I DON'T?

Panel 5: IT'S A YARMULKE. HE WEARS IT AS A GESTURE OF HUMILITY.

MALLETT

Panel 6: BUT THIS IS A DETROIT LIONS HAT.

DIFFERENT KIND OF HUMILITY.

Panel 7: YOU KNOW, FRAZZ, I DON'T THINK I'VE EVER SEEN YOU WEAR A HAT.

MAY I?

Panel 8: MALLETT

Panel 10: YOU HAVEN'T SEEN "HAT HEAD" UNTIL YOU'VE SEEN *FRAZZ* HAT HEAD.

MRS. OLSEN, I HAVE TO GO. I HAVE AN INTERVENTRICULAR SEPTUM.

OH, DEAR!

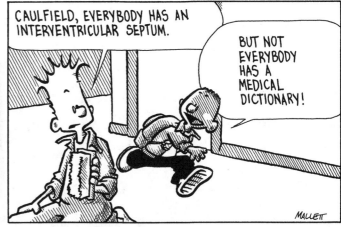

CAULFIELD, EVERYBODY HAS AN INTERVENTRICULAR SEPTUM.

BUT NOT EVERYBODY HAS A MEDICAL DICTIONARY!

MALLETT

YOU'RE MR. BURKE? OVERNIGHT LETTER. SIGN...

OKAY.

OOOOKAY.

YOU COULD HAVE JUST HANDED YOUR HOMEWORK IN LIKE THE REST OF THE CLASS, ELLI.

YOU WANT TO MAKE AN IMPRESSION, YOU SEND IT VANITY MAIL, THAT'S WHAT I HEARD.

MALLETT

SEEMS PRINCIPAL SPAETZLE DOESN'T CARE FOR MY CHOICE OF MUSIC.

HE SAYS IT'S LOUD AND VIOLENT, WITH ADULT THEMES, AND HE DOESN'T APPRECIATE THE LANGUAGE.

MALLETT

I GUESS OPERA ISN'T FOR EVERYONE.

SO TOMORROW I'M BRINGING "GAELIC BAGPIPERS"!

MRS. OLSEN ACTUALLY LOOKS HAPPY.

SHE'S A GARDENER. EVEN SHE GETS TICKLED WHEN THINGS START TO BLOOM.

MALLETT

MRS. OLSEN ACTUALLY LOOKS HAPPY.

HER BLOOMERS ARE TICKLING HER!

MRS. OLSEN SURE IS GEEKED ABOUT HER DAFFODILS.

IT'S FUNNY. CLEARLY, SHE'S A PATIENT GARDENER.

AND YET SHE DOESN'T SEEM SO PATIENT AROUND ME.

MALLETT

MAYBE HER DAFFODILS NEVER GLUED HER COFFEE CUP TO HER DESK CALENDAR.

WELL, THAT SEEMS AWFULLY ARBITRARY.

FRAZZ SAID YOU LIKE GARDENING!

MM HMM.

MALLETT

CAREFULLY COAXING PROMISE AND POTENTIAL TOWARD FULLY FORMED BEAUTY.

YES!

THEN WHY DOES TEACHING MAKE YOU GRUMPY? IT'S THE SAME THING.

...THEN SHE STARTED TALKING ABOUT PINCHING THE HEADS OFF PETUNIAS, AND I SPLIT.

I LEFT A GARDENING GIFT ON MRS. OLSEN'S DESK. BUT DID SHE APPRECIATE IT? NOOOO!

MAYBE IF I HAD EXPLAINED JUST HOW GOOD THESE THINGS ARE FOR THE SOIL...

MAYBE IF YOU HAD PUT THE EARTHWORMS IN SOME SORT OF CONTAINER.

OH, YOU HEARD.

I'M THE JANITOR, CAULFIELD.

ARE YOU OKAY, CHRISTY? YOU'VE BEEN STANDING THERE ALL RECESS.

I'M PRACTICING.

PRACTICING?

BASEBALL.

YOU KNOW, SOME PEOPLE MIGHT ARGUE...

THOSE WOULD BE THE SAME PEOPLE WHO ALWAYS PUT ME IN RIGHT FIELD.

YOU'RE RUNNING HERE?

SURE. WHY NOT?

WELL, THIS IS THE EXACT SAME ROUTE YOU BIKE TO WORK ALL WEEK.

HUH. WHAT WAS I THINKING?

MISS PLAINWELL! FANCY RUNNING INTO YOU!

THIRD SATURDAY IN A ROW!

FRAZZ, I'M TAKING A SURVEY.

OH BOY!

IF YOU COULD HAVE LUNCH WITH ANY PERSON, LIVING OR DEAD, WHO WOULD YOU CHOOSE?

MISS PLAINWELL.

YOU NEED HELP.

HEY. IT WAS HER OR MARK TWAIN, AND SHE'S GOT A WAY NICER SMILE.

YOU'D CHOOSE MISS PLAINWELL OVER MARK TWAIN?

I'M SHY, OKAY?

MISS PLAINWELL, IF YOU COULD HAVE LUNCH WITH ANY PERSON, LIVING OR DEAD, WHO WOULD YOU CHOOSE?

MARK TWAIN.

GIVE IT UP, FRAZZ.

BUT I'M NOT CHANGING MY MIND. I'M JUST MAKING SCHEDULING SUGGESTIONS.

CARRIE, I'M TAKING A SURVEY.

IF YOU COULD HAVE LUNCH WITH ANYONE, LIVING OR DEAD, WHO WOULD YOU CHOOSE?

MY GRANDPA. I REALLY MISS HIM.

EVEN IF THAT DOES MEAN EATING AT THE BLANDY DANDY BUFFET.

IN HEAVEN, THERE ARE NO POLYPS.

I NEED TO EXERCISE MORE, BUT I DON'T HAVE TIME.

I JUST EXERCISE DURING WORK HOURS.

WHAT?!

EXAMPLE: DO YOU KNOW JUST HOW MANY CALORIES A FLOOR BUFFER BURNS?

I THOUGHT YOU DIDN'T HAVE TIME TO EXERCISE TODAY.

MR. SPAETZLE IS BUFFING THE FLOORS FOR ME.

MALLETT

SO, TODAY I HOSTED "OPEN MIKE HOUR."

OPEN MICROPHONE?

MALLETT

OPEN MICROSCOPE. KIDS COULD BRING AN ITEM OF THEIR CHOICE AND WE'D STUDY IT UNDER THE MICROSCOPE.

AND?

WE STUDIED FOUR SQUISHED BUGS, A WAD OF GUM, HALF A WORM, A GOOBER AND SOMETHING UNIDENTIFIABLE FROM THE LOADING DOCK.

SOUNDS EDUCATIONAL.

I KNOW I LEARNED NOT TO DO OPEN MIKE TOO CLOSE TO LUNCH.

WEAK-SIDE HOOK SHOT, ONE EYE CLOSED, INTO THE WIND, BANKED OFF THE SWINGSET AND THROUGH THE HOOP.

OH, PLEASE, FRAZZ.

MALLETT

YOU GUYS CAN'T HIT A LAY-UP WITH A LADDER!

IT LOOKS BETTER WHEN YOU MISS THE IMPOSSIBLE ONES.

THANK YOU, "AIR" QUIXOTE.

Panel 1:
MR. BURKE, IF RIVERVIEW OFFERED YOU MORE MONEY, WOULD YOU TEACH THERE?

Panel 2:
THE PAY'S THE SAME ALL OVER TOWN. BESIDES, I LIKE IT HERE.

WHY?

Panel 3:
LARGELY MR. SPAETZLE. HE'S A GOOD MAN, AND HE STAYS OUT OF THE WAY AND LETS ME TEACH.

Panel 4:
SO IT'S NOT THE MONEY, IT'S THE PRINCIPAL.

THERE YOU GO.

Panel 5:
"So much depends upon a red wheelbarrow..."
— William Carlos Williams

MALLETT

Panel 6:
"...they sowed their isn't they reaped their same sun moon stars rain..."
— e.e. cummings

MALLETT

Panel 7:
"Get it on
Bang a gong
Get it on"
— T. Rex

POETRY DOESN'T HAVE TO MAKE SENSE TO BE COOL.

Panel 8:
I WISH I WASN'T BORN WHEN I WAS.

Panel 9:
OH, HANNA. I KNOW THE WORLD IS SCARY, BUT IT'S ALWAYS BEEN SCARY, AND PEOPLE STILL...

WHAT ARE YOU TALKING ABOUT?

MALLETT

Panel 10:
I'M UPSET BECAUSE I'M IN THE SECOND GRADE IN A YEAR WHEN CINCO DE MAYO FALLS ON A SUNDAY!

Panel 11:
OH. WHEN THAT HAPPENS, MRS. TREVINO JUST DOES THE GORDITA CELEBRATION ON MONDAY.

OKAY! NEVER MIND!

Fr 33 by J.E. Mallett

DO YOU EVER HAVE THAT DREAM WHERE...?

I'M HAVING IT NOW.

YOU KNOW HOW WHEN YOU'RE FALLING ASLEEP YOUR LEG WILL SPAZ AND YOU WAKE YOURSELF UP?

THAT'S CALLED "HYPNAGOGIC MYOCLONUS," AND NO ONE IS SURE WHY IT HAPPENS.

SOME SCIENTISTS THINK IT'S THE BRAIN LETTING GO OF MOTOR FUNCTIONS...

... KIND OF LIKE HAPPY HOUR FOR YOUR MUSCLES.

OTHERS SAY THAT WHEN YOUR MUSCLES RELAX TOO FAST, PRIMITIVE PARTS OF YOUR BRAIN INTERPRET IT AS A FALLING SENSATION, AND YOU LURCH TO KEEP YOUR BALANCE.

I GO WITH THE THEORY THAT WE'RE JUST SUSCEPTIBLE TO NOISES AND MOTION THEN, ESPECIALLY IF WE KNOW WE SHOULDN'T BE DOZING OFF IN THE FIRST PLACE.

MALLETT

AND THIS EXPERIMENT SUPPORTS YOUR THESIS HOW?

WELL, THIS PART IS JUST RESEARCH FOR RESEARCH'S SAKE.

I COULD STAY HERE, AMID FAMILIARITY AS REASSURING AS IT IS STIFLING.

MALLETT

OR CROSS OVER TO THE UNKNOWN, ITS RISKS AND REWARDS IN GREATER—BUT ASSUREDLY UNEQUAL—AMOUNTS.

I SAID, LOOK BOTH WAYS BEFORE YOU CROSS THE STREET.

OH. I THOUGHT YOU SAID SEE THINGS BOTH WAYS.

HEY FRAZZ, HOW OLD ARE YOU?

AS PAUL SIMON ONCE SANG, "OLDER THAN I ONCE WAS, YOUNGER THAN I'LL BE."

AWESOME! WE'RE THE SAME AGE!

THAT'S WHAT MRS. OLSEN TOLD ME AFTER THE ERASER FIGHT.

MALLETT

YOU LOOK AWFUL, CAULFIELD.

MY SUPPER KEPT ME UP ALL NIGHT.

WHAT'D YOU HAVE? SOMETHING FATTY? SOMETHING SPICY?

SOMETHING LIKE EIGHT CANS OF COKE.

MALLETT

THAT WAS SUPPER?!

I'M GOING TO MISS THAT BABY SITTER...

I WISH ART PROJECTS WEREN'T SO MESSY.

MAKE A SMOCK. BUM AN OLD SHIRT FROM YOUR DAD AND PUT IT ON BACKWARD.

I TRIED THAT. I KEPT BUMPING INTO THINGS.

MALLETT

OKAY, HOODED SWEATSHIRTS YOU CAN WEAR FRONTWARD.

PEOPLE NEED TO TELL ME THESE THINGS UP FRONT.

WHY DO WE HAVE TO TAKE ART? I DON'T HAVE ANY TALENT FOR ART.

I WASN'T TALENTED AT MATH, AND I HAD TO STUDY THAT.

I THOUGHT YOU WERE REALLY GOOD AT MATH.

I AM.

NOW.

MALLETT

CHECKMATE.

I'M ALSO NO GOOD AT DEBATE.

ART IS TOO HARD, FRAZZ!

TALK TO ME.

I NEVER KNOW HOW TO START!

I GUESS I'D START WHERE ALL GOOD ARTISTS START.

BY APPLYING FOR A GRANT?

BY SKETCHING. GRANTS PLAY HAVOC WITH YOUR INDEPENDENCE.

MALLETT

IF ASTRONAUTS EVER BUILD A COLONY ON MARS...

MALLETT

WILL THEY BE ABLE TO USE EARTHMOVING EQUIPMENT?

I MEANT, WERE THERE ANY QUESTIONS THAT HAVE ANYTHING TO DO WITH MATH.

FRAZZ SAYS EVERYTHING HAS SOMETHING TO DO WITH MATH.

MARIAH SAID YOU HAD SOME COOL DOLLS.

THESE AREN'T DOLLS! GEEZ!

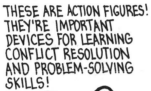

THESE ARE ACTION FIGURES! THEY'RE IMPORTANT DEVICES FOR LEARNING CONFLICT RESOLUTION AND PROBLEM-SOLVING SKILLS!

MALLETT

AND HOW GOES TODAY'S EXERCISE?

CAPTAIN COURAGE HAS PULLED OFF MALICIOUS MAN'S LEG AND IS BEATING HIM OVER THE HEAD WITH IT.

FRAZZ, DID YOU HAPPEN TO FIND ANYTHING... "INTERESTING" IN THE TRASH?

MALLETT

HOW INTERESTING?

VERY INTERESTING.

COULD YOU BE MORE SPECIFIC?

NO.

THE LAST TIME YOU DID THIS FOR SHOW AND TELL, YOU FLUNKED ANYWAY.

I'D RATHER GO DOWN SWINGING.

I'VE BEEN LOOKING FORWARD TO SUMMER VACATION ALL YEAR.

NOW THE LONG WEEKEND GIVES ME A SORT OF SNEAK PREVIEW...

AND I'M BORED.

KIND OF GOOFS WITH ANY NOTION OF IMMORTALITY, DOESN'T IT?

NOW, WHY BRING UP DEATH ON A PERFECTLY GOOD MEMORIAL DAY?

MALLETT

WHAT DO YOU SUPPOSE IT WOULD BE LIKE IF EVERYONE WAS IMMORTAL?

BORING.

BORING?

DEATH GETS PEOPLE OFF THEIR DUFFS. WITHOUT DEATH, THERE WOULD BE NO ART, NO RELIGION, NO LITERATURE...

NO NEED TO REPRODUCE

MY DAD SAYS HE'S NOT SURE THAT WAS WORTH THE EFFORT ANYWAY.

MALLETT

HOLD IT. ARE YOU SAYING DEATH CAUSES RELIGION?

ONLY SORT OF.

DEATH BREEDS FEAR AND UNCERTAINTY, AND THOSE BREED DOUBT. DOUBT FUELS A SEARCH FOR MEANING,

SO I'D SAY DOUBT IS ESSENTIAL TO RELIGION.

MALLETT

THEN CAN YOU EXPLAIN WHY SO MANY RELIGIONS DEMAND UNQUESTIONING DEVOTION?

I DOUBT IT.

SINCE I CAN'T LIVE FOREVER, I'VE DECIDED I'D LIKE TO BE REMEMBERED FOREVER.

GOOD MAN!

MR. SPAETZLE SAYS MY PERMANENT RECORD IS THE THICKEST HE'S EVER SEEN.

GOOD START!

MALLETT

WHAT IF WE LIVED TO BE A THOUSAND YEARS OLD?

A LIFESPAN'S A LIFESPAN. I DOUBT YOU'D NOTICE THE DIFFERENCE.

EXCEPT THE SEASONS WOULD CHANGE EVERY TIME YOU TURNED AROUND.

MALLETT

KIND OF LIKE LIVING IN THE MIDWEST.

PLUS YOU'D ABSOLUTELY HAVE TO MAX OUT YOUR 401(k).

MY GRANDPA USED TO SAY THAT YEARS FLY BY, BUT A MOMENT LASTS FOREVER.

MALLETT

WHAT MOMENT?

ANY MOMENT. THIS MOMENT.

WELL, THAT'S NO GOOD.

WHY? THIS IS A NICE MOMENT.

I HAVE TO GO TO THE BATHROOM.

SO DID GRANDPA, USUALLY. I THINK THERE ARE PROVISIONS.

ANGELA LOST AN EARRING AND WE THOUGHT MAYBE IT GOT SWEPT UP.

YOU COULD HAVE JUST ASKED.

WE DIDN'T WANT TO BE A BOTHER.

MALLETT

HERE'S MY REPORT ON "IVANHOE," MR. BURKE!

MIKEY, THIS IS JUST ONE SENTENCE. I ASKED FOR A PARAGRAPH.

A SENTENCE IS NOT A PARAGRAPH.

IN USA TODAY, IT IS.

DID YOU TELL HIM USA TODAY DIDN'T EXIST IN IVANHOE'S TIME?

SURE, NOW HE SUGGESTS IT.

MALLETT

WHEN I SAID WRITE A PARAGRAPH, I WAS THINKING OF SOMETHING A LITTLE LONGER.

WELL, YOU WEREN'T SPECIFIC.

I AM NOW: 100 WORDS.

OH, SO NOW IT'S A WRITING PROJECT AND A MATH ASSIGNMENT?

MALLETT

HE SAID SOMETHING ABOUT CROSS-TRAINING, BUT IT SOUNDED TO ME LIKE "JUST DO IT."

WANT SOME RASPBERRIES, CAULFIELD?

NO, THANKS. WAY TOO STRONG.

TOO STRONG? RASPBERRIES?

KIDS ARE WAY MORE SENSITIVE TO TASTE THAN ADULTS ARE, FRAZZ.

YOU PUT SUGAR ON YOUR COCOA FROSTIES.

EXACTLY! I'VE GOT TO HIDE THAT CRISPY RICE TASTE.

MALLETT

SO I WROTE A COMPUTER PROGRAM THAT MADE A TYPEFACE OUT OF MY HANDWRITING.

BUT I USED THREE ROTATING SAMPLES OF EACH LETTER SO IT DIDN'T *LOOK* LIKE A TYPEFACE.

MALLETT

FINALLY, I MADE 50 COPIES OF MY SENTENCE AND HANDED IT IN.

WHAT SENTENCE?

"I WILL NOT TAKE SHORTCUTS."

SOUNDS LIKE A LESSON.

MRS. OLSEN, WHAT DOES IT MEAN IF YOU'RE NESCIENT?

I HAVEN'T A CLUE.

MALLETT

I THINK SHE JUST GOT LUCKY.

YOU NEVER KNOW.

SO THE GUY WHO WROTE "THE GODFATHER" MUST HAVE BEEN SOME BIG MAFIA DON.

ACTUALLY, HE SWORE HE NEVER EVEN MET A MOBSTER.

HE JUST MADE THAT STUFF UP?

THAT'S SORT OF THE IDEA.

YEAH, WELL, TRY THAT WITH YOUR SCIENCE PROJECT, AND...

BIOLOGY IS CONSIDERED NONFICTION.

MALLETT

I'LL BET YOUR CLASS JUST DID THAT PLANT CIRCULATION EXPERIMENT.

...THE ONE WHERE YOU WATCH A STALK OF CELERY SOAK UP RED FOOD COLORING.

HOW DID YOU KNOW?

BECAUSE AFTERWARD EVERYBODY FEEDS THEIR RED CELERY TO MY GUINEA PIG.

THAT'S WHY HE'S TUBBY AND LOOKS LIKE HE'S WEARING LIPSTICK.

I THOUGHT YOU WERE MAKING FUN OF MRS. OLSEN.

MALLETT

I CAN'T BELIEVE YOU NEVER DID YOUR SCIENCE EXPERIMENT.

I KNEW HOW IT WAS GOING TO TURN OUT, SO I JUST WENT AHEAD AND WROTE THE REPORT.

YOU NEVER KNOW HOW THINGS WILL TURN OUT!

THEN WHY HAVEN'T YOU ASKED MISS PLAINWELL FOR A DATE?

MALLETT

AW, SHE'D NEVER... ARE YOU CHANGING THE SUBJECT?

NOPE. BUT I BET YOU'RE ABOUT TO.

MY FATHER'S GIFTS ARE GREAT BUT THIS
I CANNOT OVERSTATE:
HIS GREATEST COUP IS THAT HE'S WHO
I CHOOSE TO EMULATE.

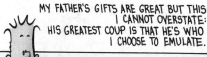

I TRY TO BE THE MAN THAT HE
CAN BE WHEN LIFE'S A TRIAL,
OR SIMULATE (SHOULD LIFE DICTATE)
A TOTAL JUVENILE.

HE'S GOT AN EAR THAT HELPS ME HEAR
THE WORLD'S A SYMPHONY;
A SPARROW'S CHIRP, A HARLEY'S BURP,
A CAT STUCK IN A TREE.

HE'S GOT AN EYE THAT SHOWS ME WHY
THE WORLD'S A MASTERPIECE,
FROM SUNSET HUES TO BIRD'S-EYE VIEWS
TO PUDDLES TRIMMED WITH GREASE.

HIS NEED TO READ AND YEARN TO LEARN
GO WITH HIM EVERYWHERE;
I LIVE THAT WAY AND END EACH DAY
MUCH MORE—AND LESS—AWARE.

BUT THOUGH
I TAKE HIS LEAD
IN OH
SO MANY WAYS
AND SORTS

THE HOMAGE STOPS
AT ARGYLE SOCKS
WITH PLAID
BERMUDA SHORTS.

WE NEED ONE MORE COACH FOR SUMMER SQUIRTS BASEBALL.

NO.

SO THAT'S A YES.

HOW IS THAT A YES?

YOU PAUSED.

I INHALED!

TIMING IS EVERYTHING.

BURKE, I'D LOVE TO COACH SUMMER SQUIRTS BASEBALL, BUT...

NO BUTS.

I DON'T KNOW ANYTHING ABOUT BASEBALL!

YOU DON'T KNOW ANYTHING ABOUT BASKETBALL, BUT HERE YOU ARE.

UNNECESSARY BLUNTNESS! FIVE YARDS!

WHO ELSE IS COACHING SUMMER SQUIRTS BASEBALL?

LET'S SEE: JANE PLAINWELL,

DO YOU THINK SHE'LL WEAR A PONYTAIL?

I'M SORRY. AM I GOING TOO FAST?

ALL RIGHT, BURKE. I'LL DO IT. I'LL COACH A BASEBALL TEAM.

SWEET!

I LIKE THE COACHES, I LOVE THE KIDS...

I MEAN WHAT'S THE DOWNSIDE?

MY UMPIRE HAT WON'T FIT OVER MY BUN.

MALLETT

HEY, FRAZZ! I HEARD YOU'RE COACHING SUMMER SQUIRTS BASEBALL!

YUP!

I HOPE I'M ON YOUR TEAM!

YOU ARE.

MALLETT

REALLY? DID YOU HAVE TO, LIKE, GIVE UP A DRAFT PICK?

ACTUALLY, I GAINED A FEW.

OH.

DID YOU REALLY BOOBY TRAP THIRD BASE WITH HONEY LAST YEAR?

SINCE WHEN DID I START GETTING "POODLE FANCY" MAGAZINE?

SINCE WHEN DID I START GETTING "MONSTER TRUCK MONTHLY"?

SINCE WHEN DID I START GETTING "MUSCLE AND FITNESS ILLUSTRATED"?

SINCE WHEN DID THE LIBRARIAN START CUTTING THE "BILL ME LATER" ADS OUT OF THE MAGAZINES?

MALLETT

HEY, FRAZZ! DID YOU FIX THE CLOCK IN MRS. OLSEN'S ROOM?

I CHECKED IT.

IT KEEPS PERFECT TIME.

MALLETT

DUH! THAT'S EXACTLY THE PROBLEM!

THE LAST DAY OF SCHOOL IS THE CRUELEST.

KNOW WHAT I'M LOOKING FORWARD TO? NO HOMEWORK!

DON'T YOU HAVE A SUMMER READING LIST?

WELL, YEAH. BUT I FIGURED I'D KNOCK THAT OFF OVER THE LONG WEEKEND.

MALLETT

YOU'LL BE ON VACATION. WHY WAIT UNTIL THE 4TH OF JULY WEEKEND?

NO, NO, LABOR DAY. I NEED THAT SENSE OF URGENCY.

SO LET'S TALK ABOUT SENSE...

MAN, I AM SO READY TO BE DONE.

WHEN MY MOM WANTS TO GO HOME EARLY, SHE SKIPS BREAKFAST AND GOES STRAIGHT TO WORK.

THEN SHE WORKS THROUGH LUNCH

THEN SHE'S SO TIRED AND INEFFICIENT SHE ENDS UP WORKING UNTIL 6:00.

MALLETT

AM I SUPPOSED TO BE LEARNING SOMETHING HERE?

I DON'T KNOW. MY MOM DOESN'T.

Panel 1: WELCOME TO SUMMER SQUIRTS BASEBALL! IF YOU'RE A COUGAR, COME WITH ME.

Panel 2: MISS PLAINWELL WILL BE COACHING THE BEARS. MR. HACKER WILL BE COACHING THE BULLDOGS. AND FRAZZ WILL...

Panel 3: OK, YOU CAN'T CALL YOUR TEAM THE FIGHTING MARTHA STEWARTS.

BUT I WANTED SOMETHING INTIMIDATING.

CAN WE EMBROIDER OUR HATS?

Panel 4: DID YOU KNOW MADELEINE ZHU WAS ON OUR TEAM?

Panel 5: SURE. SHE WAS MY FIRST PICK.

WHAT?

Panel 6: WHY WOULD YOU CHOOSE HER FIRST? SHE'S ALWAYS THE LAST ONE PICKED FOR KICKBALL AT RECESS!

Panel 7: THAT'S WHY.

GREAT. WE'LL BE THE ORIGINAL METS, ONLY WITH GOOD KARMA.

Panel 8: YOU PICKED JESSE FOR OUR BASEBALL TEAM? HIS DAD IS TOTALLY OBNOXIOUS AND BOSSY!

Panel 9: I HEARD. I ALSO HEARD HE OWNS THE CHEVROLET DEALERSHIP.

Panel 10: SO?

I MAY HAVE HINTED IT COULD BE TIME TO REPLACE MY CHEVETTE.

STILL DOING A GREAT JOB OUT THERE, MR. FRAZZ!

WELL, YOU'RE AT WORK EARLY.

IT'S ELEVEN O'CLOCK.

IT'S SUMMER VACATION.

AH. AND YOU'RE EIGHT.

GOOD TO SEE SLEEP DEPRIVATION HASN'T HURT YOUR PROBLEM-SOLVING SKILLS.

WHY DON'T YOU SLEEP IN DURING THE SUMMER, FRAZZ?

I STILL HAVE TO WORK.

BUT YOU CAN SET YOUR OWN HOURS, RIGHT?

EXACTLY! THAT'S WHY I START AT 5 A.M. THEN I FINISH IN PLENTY OF TIME TO DO OTHER...

Z

ON THE OTHER HAND, I'LL HAVE PLENTY OF ENERGY TO TEASE HIM ONCE HE SNAPS TO.

WHY IS THAT PLANT ALL PRICKLY?

SURVIVAL OF THE FITTEST.

OVER THOUSANDS OF YEARS, IT DEVELOPED AN UNFRIENDLY NATURE SO IT DIDN'T GET PICKED OR EATEN.

WELL, I DON'T THINK BEING PRICKLY IS ANY WAY TO SURVIVE.

THAT WAS SO CLOSE TO BEING TOUCHING.

MR. DARWIN, MEET MR. WEED-B-GON!

88

LOOK AT THE GUY ACROSS THE STREET.

I'M TRYING NOT TO.

WHY ON EARTH WOULD HE PUTTER AROUND HIS YARD IN LONG PANTS BUT NO SHIRT?

MAYBE HE DOESN'T LIKE THE WAY HIS LEGS LOOK.

EXCEPT THAT I DOUBT HE CAN SEE HIS LEGS.

YOU MAY HAVE A POINT.

MALLETT

UNBELIEVABLE! THE GUY ACROSS THE STREET HAS A TINY LAWN, AND HE'S USING A RIDING MOWER!

IT'S ALL THE MORE PATHETIC SINCE HE COULD CLEARLY USE THE EXERCISE!

THAT FAR CORNER IS A GOOD WORKOUT, EVEN WITH A LITTLE TRACTOR.

THAT'S WHERE THE BEES' NEST IS.

WOW! LOOK AT HIM GO!

MALLETT

ICK! WHY DO WE HAVE TO HAVE MOSQUITOES?

THEY'RE AN IMPORTANT SOURCE OF FOOD.

FOR WHAT?

BATS. TOADS.

MALLETT

ICK! WHY DO WE NEED BATS AND TOADS?

TO EAT THE MOSQUITOES.

I'M SO PROUD TO BE AT THE TOP OF THAT FOOD CHAIN.

DON'T FLATTER YOURSELF. WE'RE THE ONES GETTING MUNCHED HERE.

WHO ARE WE PLAYING TODAY, MR. HACKER?

FRAZZ'S TEAM.

I KNOW, BUT WHAT...

THEY'RE STILL TRYING TO THINK OF A SCARY NAME.

THE COFFEE BREATH!

WE WANT INTIMIDATING SCARY, NOT GROSS SCARY.

THE STORY PROBLEMS!

THE NOISY FURNACE IN THE DARK BASEMENT!

TODAY, WE'RE PLAYING THE BULLDOG.

YOU MEAN BULLDOGS.

NO, JUST BULLDOG. I GUESS COACH HACKER GOT PUSHY AND EVERYBODY BUT AARON QUIT.

HE'S TAKING US ON ALL BY HIMSELF? WOW.

THAT SAYS A LOT ABOUT AARON.

UNFORTUNATELY, IT SAYS MORE ABOUT US.

WHICH END OF THIS THING DO YOU HOLD AGAIN?

MADELEINE NEEDS EITHER A LIGHTER HELMET OR A SHORTER BAT.

I DON'T KNOW. WE'RE TALKING SERIOUSLY ELUSIVE STRIKE ZONE.

DO WE NEED TO WORK ON NOT BEING AFRAID OF THE BALL?

LET ME BAT IN CATCHER'S GEAR AND WE'LL TALK.

I HIT THE BALL!

I HIT THE BALL
I HIT THE BALL
I HIT THE BALL
I HIT THE BALL!

I HIT THE BALL!

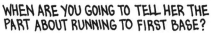

WHEN ARE YOU GOING TO TELL HER THE PART ABOUT RUNNING TO FIRST BASE?

ONE TRIUMPH AT A TIME, CAULFIELD.

GOOD GAME, FRAZZ.

HEY, YOUR TEAM DID GREAT, CONSIDERING IT WAS JUST ONE GUY.

YEAH. WELL. I GUESS I LEARNED A LESSON WHEN EVERYBODY QUIT. YOU CAN'T COACH LITTLE KIDS LIKE COLLEGE PLAYERS.

WHOA.

ALTHOUGH WE DID GO INTO EXTRA INNINGS.

THERE'S OUR OLD MR. HACKER.

WHAT'S THIS?

NEW LIBRARY BOOKS!

BUT I DIDN'T BUDGET FOR NEW LIBRARY BOOKS.

YOU DON'T SAY.

I HEARD THAT SONG YOU WROTE FOR GRAY GHOST PORTER WENT GOLD.

YOU DON'T SAY.

MALLETT

"HOP ON POP," "JUMANJI," "TUESDAY," "GO DOG GO," "DANGEROUS DAN"...

"JAMES AND THE GIANT PEACH," "RAMONA THE PEST," "STUART LITTLE"...

"THE GRAPES OF WRATH," "A FAREWELL TO ARMS"...

I THINK MR. SPAETZLE'S ON TO YOU.

HE'S GETTING FASTER.

MALLETT

IT WAS YOU WHO BOUGHT US ALL THOSE LIBRARY BOOKS?

BUSTED!

I DO THAT WHENEVER ONE OF MY SONGS SELLS WELL. IT'S HOW I GIVE BACK.

WHICH SONG? THIS SONG?

... AND MAKE AMENDS TO THE ENGLISH LANGUAGE, IF NECESSARY.

"AIN'T GOT NO GIT GO NO MO"?

MALLETT

FRAZZ, I WISH YOU'D CHECKED WITH ME BEFORE YOU BOUGHT US SOME OF THOSE BOOKS.

WHAT'S THE PROBLEM?

CONTENT! JUST WHAT AM I SUPPOSED TO DO WITH SOMETHING LIKE "CATCH-22"?

WELL, JOSEPH HELLER WROTE IT, SO I GUESS I'D FILE IT UNDER "H"

THE BOOK IS VIOLENT AND DISTURBING!

...JUST A FEW STEPS FROM "GRIMM'S FAIRY TALES," AS LONG AS YOU'RE LOOKING FOR DISTURBING BOOKS.

MALLETT

WE CAN'T PUT "CATCH-22" IN AN ELEMENTARY SCHOOL LIBRARY.

BUT IT'S GOOD!

IT'S INAPPROPRIATE! IT'S GOT RUDE LANGUAGE, BIZARRE CHARACTERS AND, BENEATH THE WARPED HUMOR, A FAIRLY ADVANCED THEME!

WHAT KID IS GOING TO WANT TO READ THAT?

PRETTY MUCH ALL OF THEM, IF THEY COULD HEAR YOU DESCRIBE IT THAT WAY.

MALLETT

FRAZZ, I'M GRATEFUL THAT YOU BOUGHT THE SCHOOL ALL THOSE BOOKS.

BOOKS

BUT PLEASE RUN THESE THINGS PAST ME! DON'T IGNORE THE SYSTEM!

LOOK! "MIKE MULLIGAN AND HIS STEAM SHOVEL"!

OOH!

MALLETT

YOU ORDER "MIKE MULLIGAN" EVERY TIME, DON'T YOU?

THAT'S SO THE SYSTEM WILL IGNORE ME.

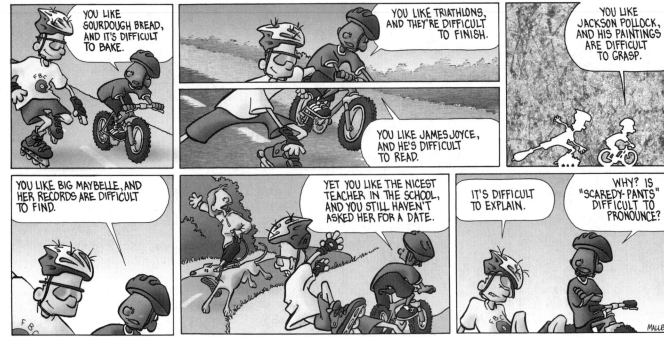

Panel 1:
DID FRAZZ'S TEAM EVER COME UP WITH A NAME?

A NICE ONE: "FRAZZ'S OUTFIT."

Panel 2:
BUT I THOUGHT THEY WANTED TO NAME THEMSELVES AFTER SOMETHING SCARY.

HUH.

Panel 3:
WHAT'S SO SCARY ABOUT MY OUTFIT?

OH, PLEASE, FRAZZ. A HAWAIIAN SHIRT AND PLAID SHORTS?

Panel 4:
GEEZ, FRAZZ. I NEVER EXPECTED YOU TO BE ALL NERVOUS ABOUT A BASEBALL GAME.

WE'RE PLAYING THE BEARS.

Panel 5:
SO? THEY'VE GOT THE SAME RECORD AS US.

MISS *PLAINWELL'S* BEARS.

Panel 6:
IT'S A BASEBALL GAME, NOT A BARN DANCE!

AND SHE'S WEARING A PONYTAIL!

Panel 7:
I THINK WE NEED TO CALL THE GAME OFF.

WHY? BECAUSE YOU'VE GOT THE HOTS FOR THE OPPOSING COACH AND YOUR STOMACH IS BUBBLING LIKE A POT OF BAD BURGOO?

Panel 8:
I WAS THINKING RAIN.

IT HASN'T RAINED IN TWO WEEKS.

Panel 9:
IT RAINED ALL SPRING, AND THE MOSQUITOES ARE REALLY BAD.

YOUR TEAM BATS FIRST, CASANOVA.

WHY
COACHES
ARE
GROWN-UPS:

WHY
TEAMMATES
ARE
KIDS:

AFTER THE GAME, ARE YOU GOING TO GIVE MISS PLAINWELL A CONGRATULATORY KISS?

CAULFIELD! THAT'S NOT HOW BASEBALL WORKS!

THAT'S WHAT MR. HACKER TRIED TO DO LAST WEEK.

WHAT?

UNTIL SHE SAID SOMETHING ABOUT A CONGRATULATORY BASEBALL BEING PUSHED UP HIS NOSE.

MALLETT

INFATUATION: UP. INTIMIDATION: WAY UP.

IF YOU'RE JUST GOING TO STAND THERE, CAN I GO ARGUE A CALL OR SOMETHING?

JUST ASK MISS PLAINWELL FOR A DATE, CHICKEN MAN. SOMETHING LOW-KEY. TAKE BOTH TEAMS TO THE DAIRY QUEEN AFTER THE GAME.

THAT'S A GOOD IDEA.

IT'S AN AWESOME IDEA!

UM... HOW AWESOME?

WELL, SHE SAID YES.

MALLETT

CAULFIELD!

BUT ONLY IF YOU GO RUNNING WITH HER SATURDAY.

I gaze at the lightning bugs circling above in their flashily luminous quest for some lovin'

MALLETT

and think that I'm grateful that we're not the ones

to have what's in our hearts be betrayed by our buns.

I CAN'T BELIEVE YOU DIDN'T KNOW MISS PLAINWELL LIKES YOU.

I CAN'T BELIEVE MYSELF.

TOMORROW, I GO RUNNING WITH JANE PLAINWELL— MY IDEA OF THE PERFECT DATE.

TODAY, I'M SO NERVOUS I—WHAT?—YES! I GO FOR A LONG RUN.

I'LL BE POOPED TOMORROW.

I CAN'T BELIEVE MYSELF.

...I WAS SO KEYED UP ABOUT GOING OUT WITH YOU TOMORROW, I HAD TO GO FOR A LONG RUN TODAY.

ME, TOO.

YOU, TOO? BUT YOU'RE A GODDESS! I'M A DOOFUS!

A DOOFUS? FRAZZ, I'VE WANTED TO GO OUT WITH YOU SINCE I STARTED TEACHING HERE.

YOU KNOW, THE TRACTION'S AWFUL UP HERE.

I'M IN NO HURRY.

FRAZZ, EVERYBODY WANTS TO KNOW HOW YOUR DATE WITH MISS PLAINWELL WENT.

OH, HI, CAULFIELD.

PRETTY GOOD!

SCHOOL CAN'T START TOMORROW! I'M NOT FINISHED WITH SUMMER YET!

I HAVE THINGS TO DISCOVER! BOOKS TO READ! GAMES TO PLAY!

THAT'S WHAT GOES ON IN SCHOOL.

IT WORKS SO MUCH BETTER ON A VOLUNTEER BASIS.

MALLETT

SUMMER VACATION IS TOO SHORT! I CAN'T WAIT TILL I'M GROWN UP!

MOST GROWN-UPS HAVE TO WORK ALL SUMMER.

MALLETT

NOT ME! I'M GOING TO BE A PRO HOCKEY PLAYER!

CAREFUL. THOSE GUYS HAVE AN INCREDIBLY SHORT OFF-SEASON.

THEN I'LL PLAY FOR WASHINGTON.

EVEN THE CAPITALS MAKE THE PLAYOFFS SOMETIMES.

FRAZZ SAYS SCHOOL DIDN'T USED TO START THIS SOON.

TRUE. IN A MORE FARM-ORIENTED SOCIETY, KIDS HAD TO HELP BRING IN THE CROPS.

I HELPED MY GRANDMA WITH THE GROCERY SHOPPING YESTERDAY.

MALLETT

THAT OUGHT TO LEAVE YOU PLENTY OF ENERGY FOR SCHOOL.

CLEARLY SOMEBODY'S NEVER BRAVED SENIORS TUESDAY AT GIANTWAY.

DID YOU DO ANYTHING COOL OVER THE SUMMER?

I DID A HANDS-ON WETLAND HABITAT SURVEY.

WAY COOL! WHEN?

JUST NOW.

UH-OH. WHERE?

SO I'M OVERDUE TO UNCLOG THE STORM DRAIN IN THE PARKING LOT...

MOSTLY I FOUND WORMS AND PAPER CUPS.

MALLETT

THREE!

FIVE!

MALLETT

FOUR!

HA! SEVEN!

A SUCCESSFUL SUMMER IS MEASURED BY THE NUMBER OF HOLES WORN IN THE NUMBER OF KNEES IN THE NUMBER OF JEANS!

TWO, BUT THEY WERE HUGE!

WELL, IF YOU CAN ASSIGN READING OVER THE SUMMER, WE OUGHT TO BE ABLE TO BRING A LITTLE SUMMER BACK TO SCHOOL.

HE MAKES A DECENT POINT.

MALLETT

FRAZZ
Jeffrey A. Mallett

Means, means, the magical stuff
The more you gots, the less enough
The less enough, the more the crave
The stronger that, the worse behave
The worse behave, the fewer friends
The magicer means,
The tragicer ends.

LANDLORD GOOSE THE RENT AGAIN?

MY DAD LIKES TO TURN OUR VACATIONS INTO LEARNING OPPORTUNITIES.

THIS YEAR'S THEME WAS "CAPITALIST HEROES."

WE DROVE OUT EAST AND LOOKED AT THESE HUMONGOUS OLD MANSIONS. I'M, LIKE, WHOA!

DAD SAID THE LATE 1800s AND EARLY 1900s SAW A FEW MEN BUILD GREAT FORTUNES.

SOME GOT RICH THROUGH INVENTION AND RISK-TAKING; SOME THROUGH TREACHERY AND CORRUPTION.

SOME MADE A LOT OF OTHER PEOPLE WEALTHY; SOME KEPT A LOT OF OTHER PEOPLE POOR.

SOME MADE THE WORLD A BETTER PLACE; SOME LIVED ONLY IN THEIR OWN WORLD.

THEN THE QUIZ: DAD ASKED, "WHAT ONE TRAIT DID ALL THESE MEN HAVE IN COMMON?"

MALLETT

I SAID, WELL, THEY'RE ALL DEAD NOW.

A LEARNING OPPORTUNITY FOR YOUR DAD, NO DOUBT.

LABOR DAY IS THE CRUELEST HOLIDAY.

IT LETS YOU REALIZE SUMMER HAS SLIPPED AWAY...

MALLETT

WITHOUT GIVING YOU ENOUGH TIME TO REALLY GET IT BACK.

PLUS ALL YOU CAN GET ON TV IS THAT TELETHON.

I MIGHT KNOW WHERE YOUR SUMMER WENT.

AIR THAT'S MOVING HAS A LOWER PRESSURE THAN AIR THAT'S NOT.

SO THE STILL AIR IN THE ROOM ALWAYS PUSHES THE PING PONG BALL BACK INTO THE MOVING AIR FROM THE HAIR DRYER.

MALLETT

FRAZZ, CAN WE BORROW YOUR LEAF BLOWER?

MR. BURKE MUST BE TEACHING BERNOULLI'S PRINCIPLE AGAIN.

HOW COME MR. SPAETZLE IS THE PRINCIPAL AND YOU'RE THE JANITOR?

WELL, SOMEBODY'S GOT TO DO IT.

MALLETT

WHICH ONE?

DEPENDS ON THE DAY.

WHAT ARE YOU DOING?

FLOCCULATING MY NESTLE'S QUIK.

OKAY. WHY?

MOSTLY JUST SO I CAN SAY IT.

MALLETT

DISCOVERING A NEW WORD IS LIKE FINDING MONEY ON THE SIDEWALK!

THE SOONER YOU CAN BLOW IT, THE BETTER!

WELL, THAT'S A RIDICULOUS THING TO TEASE ME ABOUT!

MALLETT

TEASE YOU ABOUT WHAT?

USING BIG WORDS.

WHO'S DOING THAT?

ZACHARIAH VANDENMEERENDONK.

DO YOU SUPPOSE "IRONY" IS TOO BIG A WORD FOR HIM?

INDUBITABLY.

"TWINKLE TWINKLE LITTLE STAR"... "THE ABCs"... "BAA BAA BLACK SHEEP"...

HAVE YOU EVER NOTICED THEY'RE ALL THE EXACT SAME SONG?

MALLETT

SHE SAID SHE'S ALWAYS FELT THE SAME WAY ABOUT "THAT RAP STUFF."

CURIOUS WORDS FROM THE PROUD OWNER OF THE "PAULIE THE PRINCE OF POLKA" BOX SET.

I THINK YOU NEED TO TURN THE WATER PRESSURE DOWN.

REALLY? CAULFIELD JUST ASKED ME TO TURN IT UP.

FRAZZ, CAN I ASK YOU AN AWKWARD QUESTION?

OF COURSE, LUPE. THERE ARE NO AWKWARD QUESTIONS BETWEEN FRIENDS.

$$\frac{(12 \times 7) + (20 \div 5)}{(9 + 2)} =$$

THAT SOUNDS MORE LIKE A HOMEWORK QUESTION.

WELL, ISN'T THIS AWKWARD?

WHERE HAVE YOU BEEN ALL AFTERNOON?

IN THE LIBRARY WITH LUPE.

SHE CASUALLY INQUIRED IF I MIGHT KNOW OFFHAND WHAT $\frac{(12 \times 7) + (20 \div 5)}{(9 + 2)}$ WAS, AND WE WORKED IT OUT TOGETHER.

SO SHE DIDN'T GET OUT OF DOING HER HOMEWORK.

NO, BUT I GOT OUT OF SCRUBBING THE DUMPSTER!

I LIKE YOUR BLOUSE!

THANKS!

CLEARANCE, NORDFIELDS, $24.97! I LIKE YOUR... WELL, T-SHIRT.

BREAKAWAY BICYCLES, $12.

WHEN YOU WORK IN COVERALLS, ALL YOUR FASHION STATEMENTS ARE UNDER $20.

I'M JEALOUS. I THINK.

MALLETT

NOW, BEFORE THE QUIZ, ARE THERE ANY QUESTIONS? YES, CAULFIELD?

WHY DO THEY ALWAYS SELL, SAY, 50 ASPIRINS IN WHAT'S OBVIOUSLY A 100-ASPIRIN BOTTLE?

WHY DO YOU DO THAT TO MRS. OLSEN?

WELL, SHE SEEMS TO GO THROUGH A LOT OF ASPIRIN.

MALLETT

OKAY, TECHNICALLY I WASN'T RUNNING.

AND TECHNICALLY, YOU'RE NO LONGER IN THE HALLWAY.

MALLETT

FRAZZ ISN'T ACTING ALL WEIRD AROUND MISS PLAINWELL THIS YEAR.

THEY'RE KIND OF AN ITEM NOW.

HE FINALLY ASKED HER OUT?

I SORT OF ASKED HER FOR HIM. I GOT TIRED OF THE FRAIDY CAT SOAP OPERA.

GOLLY, I SURE AM SCARED OF MY VOCABULARY WORKSHEET!

SORRY. THAT I CAN LIVE WITH.

MALLETT

FRAZZ AND MISS PLAINWELL HAVE A THING?

YOU TELL ME.

THEY'VE BEEN DISAPPEARING AT LUNCH AND COMING BACK ALL FLUSHED AND BREATHLESS.

MALLETT

AW! THEY'RE SMOOCHING! HOW SWEET!

THIS IS FRAZZ AND MISS PLAINWELL, REMEMBER.

DISTANCE OR INTERVALS?

SPEED WORK. I'VE GOT A 10K RACE SATURDAY.

I CAN'T RUN TODAY. I'VE GOT A LITTLE TENDINITIS.

THAT'S OK, FRAZZ. I'M GETTING A BLISTER.

I COULD TAKE YOU TO LUNCH!

YOU GOT A PLACE IN MIND?

MALLETT

THE FOOD'S GROSS, BUT YOU CAN'T BEAT THE AMBIENCE!

TRADE YOU A FISH STICK FOR YOUR ROLL.

FRAZZ AND MISS PLAINWELL SITTIN' IN A TREE! K-I-S-S-I-N-G!

WHAT MADE YOU DECIDE TO TEACH FIRST GRADE?

ACTUALLY, I ORIGINALLY MAJORED IN JOURNALISM.

I SCORED AN INTERNSHIP WITH THE RECORD'S SPORTS DEPARTMENT!

WHEREUPON YOU DECIDED...

I NEEDED TO WORK WITH A MORE MATURE CROWD.

THANKS FOR LUNCH, FRAZZ!

PLEASURE.

I BET THE KIDS WERE TOTALLY SURPRISED TO SEE US TOGETHER.

TOTALLY!

FRIDAY THE 20TH. OKAY, TESS AND MARCO TIED IN THE FRAZZ/MISS PLAINWELL POOL.

NO WAY! MARCO ENTERED TWICE!

DID NOT!

YOU FIXED UP FRAZZ AND MISS PLAINWELL, CAULFIELD? YOU RULE!

YOU GIVE ME TOO MUCH CREDIT.

THOSE TWO ARE BLUE MOON ICE CREAM AND A WHITE SHIRT. I WAS MERELY... GRAVITY.

THAT IS A DISGUSTING ANALOGY.

I LIKE METAPHORS WHERE I'M AN UNSTOPPABLE FORCE OF NATURE.

by JEF MALLETT

I ONCE SAW B.B. KING PERFORM. THE GUY'S GOT FINGERS LIKE BRATWURSTS.

YOU'D THINK THEY WOULDN'T FIT ON THE GUITAR NECK AT ALL. AND YET, OBVIOUSLY, THEY FIT EXACTLY WHERE AND WHEN THEY NEED TO.

I ONCE SAW JEROME BETTIS PLAY FOOTBALL. THE GUY HAS AN ENGINE.

HE'S FAST ENOUGH TO RUN AWAY FROM TACKLERS, BUT HE'D JUST AS SOON BASH RIGHT THROUGH THEM.

WHAT'S UP?

WE'RE WATCHING MRS. OLSEN PARK HER BUICK.

WE HAVE A BET.

CAN I JOIN? I BET SHE MAKES IT.

MALLETT

WE'RE NOT BETTING ON *WHETHER* SO MUCH AS *HOW.*

MY CAR!

WIN.

117

IF I GOT THE RIGHT ANSWER TO A MATH PROBLEM USING A DIFFERENT METHOD THAN THE ONE MRS. OLSEN WAS TEACHING US, AM I NOT, IN FACT, RIGHT?

GEE, THAT'S A TOUGH ONE. WHAT METHOD DID YOU USE?

I GUESS YOU'D CALL IT THE PEEK-AT-THE-TEACHER'S-EDITION-ON-THE-WAY-TO-THE-BATHROOM METHOD.

MAYBE IT'S NOT SUCH A TOUGH ONE.

MALLETT

YOU'D THINK MORE BLOOD FLOW TO YOUR BRAIN WOULD MAKE IT WORK BETTER, RIGHT?

MALLETT

SO I TRIED STANDING ON MY HEAD BEFORE CLASSES TO SEE IF I LEARNED MORE.

I BET THE DRESS WAS A BAD IDEA.

THAT WAS THE FIRST THING I LEARNED!

SEE THOSE BIG KIDS, HOW THEIR PANTS FIT?

YOU'LL NEVER SEE ME WEARING MY PANTS LIKE THAT.

NO?

MY MOM ONLY BUYS ME UNDERPANTS WITH LITTLE CARTOON DUCKS ON THEM.

MY MOM DOESN'T UNDERSTAND FASHION.

OR ELSE SHE DOES.

MALLETT

YOU KNOW HOW YOU CAN PRESERVE LEAVES BY PRESSING THEM BETWEEN PAGES IN A BIG BOOK?

DID YOU KNOW IT DOESN'T WORK WITH TENTWORMS?

MALLETT

CAULFIELD, WHAT IF SOMEONE WANTS TO READ THAT?

I DOUBT IT. I USED THE CHAPTER ON MILLARD FILLMORE.

ONE: IT'S GETTING A LITTLE CHILLY.

MALLETT

TWO: YOU REALLY DON'T NEED TO GO SHIRTS AND SKINS WHEN YOU'RE PLAYING ONE-ON-ONE.

THREE: THE PLAYERS COMPRISE A WEIGHT PROBLEM AND A SERIOUS BIKER'S TAN.

REASONS ONE AND TWO WERE JUST FOR SHOW, WEREN'T THEY?

DIZZY DEAN SAID, "IT AIN'T BRAGGING IF IT'S TRUE." SIMILARLY, IT AIN'T TALKING TRASH IF IT'S TRUE.

MALLETT

INCORRECT QUOTE. HE SAID, "IT AIN'T BRAGGING IF YOU CAN *BACK IT UP*," AND I CHALLENGE YOU TO PROVE DEFINITIVELY THAT A BLIMP IN A HURRICANE IS MORE DEPENDABLE THAN MY JUMP SHOT.

REMIND ME WHY YOU TWO AREN'T LAWYERS.

LAW FIRMS DON'T TEND TO HAVE PLAYGROUNDS.

I sing a song of...

... singing songs. I play a tune of...

... playing. I write about...

... my writer's block...

WELL, THAT GOES WITHOUT SAYING.

October takes your breath away yet people seem to favor May,

which comes with bugs, humidity and rain. So why the primacy?

October means November soon while May gives way each year to June.

Alas, no matter what you do, you're judged by what comes after you.

MY DAD SAYS THAT SONG GIVES HIM HIVES.

I feed my Guinea pig and clean his pen. I fill his water bottle up and then

repeat the process daily, more or less, because I'm his superior, I guess.

Which makes me question human beings and our insatiable, obsessive lust for power.

Z

Americans hate Vegemite; Australians don't like Jif.
And natto looks like something rescued from a handkerchief.

Norwegians nosh on lutefisk from a stinky, toxic vat;
the French make gourmet feasts from stuff we wouldn't feed the cat.

One region's culture's vinegar's another's muscatel.
So why are we so proud our fries and burgers sell so well?

DO YOU MIND?

YOU'VE ALWAYS GOT LYLE WITH YOU WHEN YOU WRITE SONGS.

I WRITE BETTER WITH HIS HELP. I GUESS HE'S SORT OF MY MUSE.

I THOUGHT A MUSE WAS A BEAUTIFUL GODDESS, NOT A FUZZY RODENT WITH A TASTE FOR PORK RINDS.

YOU KNOW I CAN'T CONCENTRATE AROUND BEAUTIF— WHO'S BEEN FEEDING HIM PORK RINDS?

HOW IS LYLE YOUR MUSE? DOES HE TALK TO YOU?

DON'T BE SILLY.

ANIMALS ONLY TALK IN CARTOONS!

I DON'T GET IT.

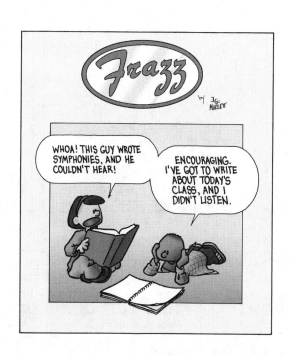

FRAZZ, CAN I BORROW YOUR SHOVEL?

SURE. WHAT FOR?

THE ANTHILL AT THE BOTTOM OF THE SLIDE.

THERE'S NOT AN ANTHILL AT THE BOTTOM OF THE SLIDE.

RIGHT. YOU DON'T EXPECT ME TO MOVE ONE THERE WITH MY BARE HANDS, DO YOU?

I TAKE IT MEAN GENE IS HOGGING THE SLIDE AGAIN.

MALLETT

I WAS READING ABOUT THIS RULE CALLED THE "GOLDEN MEAN."

IT HINTS THAT MANY THINGS IN NATURE PEAK AT THE TWO-THIRDS POINT.

LIKE, MAYBE TWO THIRDS OF THE WAY DOWN THE SLIDE, YOU REACH MAXIMUM SPEED.

MALLETT

SO IF WE SPREAD THE RUBBER CEMENT THERE, WE'RE TALKING MAXIMUM WEDGIE.

BINGO.

MEAN GENE STILL HOGGING THE SLIDE?

MEAN GENE IS SUCH A BULLY!

PSHT!

WHEN YOU'RE BOTH 30, HE'LL BE WORKING FOR YOU!

WHAT?

MAYBE I DON'T WANT TO OWN A BOO BOO BURGER FRANCHISE WHEN I'M 30.

AH. PERHAPS YOU COULD PLACE A COMPLICATED SPECIAL ORDER NOW AND THEN.

MALLETT

I GUESS I *COULD* BUY A BOO BOO BURGER FRANCHISE SOMEDAY AND BOSS MEAN GENE AROUND WHEN HIS CAREER PEAKS AT THE FRENCH FRY STATION.

BUT IF I DO SOMETHING I DON'T WANT JUST TO HOSE MEAN GENE, I'M STILL LETTING HIM MAKE MY LIFE MISERABLE.

GOOD MAN! YOU JUST FIGURED OUT WHY REVENGE IS A LOSER'S GAME.

ALTHOUGH I DON'T SEE A DOWNSIDE TO SLIPPING A DEAD FISH IN HIS DESK.

I DO.

FRAZZ, THAT SQUIRREL IS RAIDING THE BIRD FEEDER AGAIN.

MAN, HE'S CLEVER.

IF SQUIRRELS HAD OPPOSABLE THUMBS AND A LANGUAGE, THEY WOULD RUN THE COUNTRY.

MY DAD SAYS MONKEYS RUN THE COUNTRY.

YOUR DAD MIGHT WANT TO LISTEN TO A LITTLE LESS TALK RADIO.

I SKINNED MY KNEE, FRAZZ!

HANG ON. I'VE GOT JUST THE THING FOR THAT.

PROBABLY SHOULD HAVE MENTIONED THE PADLOCK ON THE FIRST AID KIT WAS RUSTED SHUT.

LOOKS TO ME LIKE HER KNEES ARE WORKING JUST FINE.

EEEEE
EEEEE

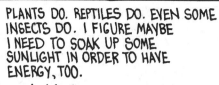
PLANTS DO. REPTILES DO. EVEN SOME INSECTS DO. I FIGURE MAYBE I NEED TO SOAK UP SOME SUNLIGHT IN ORDER TO HAVE ENERGY, TOO.

AND THAT'S WHY YOU'RE SPENDING RECESS JUST LYING THERE?

YUP.

I THOUGHT THE POINT OF RECESS WAS TO BURN ENERGY.

YOU DIDN'T NOD OFF AND FALL OUT OF YOUR CHAIR DURING A FILM STRIP ON PHOTOSYNTHESIS.

MALLETT

SO I WAS LAYING HERE AND...

LYING HERE.

HUH?

YOU "LAY" SOMETHING DOWN. YOU YOURSELF "LIE" ON SOMETHING.

WHAT IF I SAID IT DIDN'T MATTER?

THEN YOU'D BE "LYING." THOUGH YOU COULD BE "IGNORANT."

MALLETT

ENGLISH IS WAY TOO COMPLICATED.

WELL, SANSKRIT WAS ALREADY TAKEN.

DID YOU EVER REALLY THINK ABOUT HOW CATS GROOM THEMSELVES?

CAN YOU THINK OF ANYTHING AS GROSS AS LICKING DIRT OFF OF HAIR?

THAT TOOTSIE POP YOU FOUND IN YOUR JACKET POCKET FROM LAST SPRING IS GIVING ME SOME IDEAS.

WHAT? IT STILL HAD MOST OF ITS WRAPPER.

MALLETT

SOME PEOPLE SAY YOU'RE OLD WHEN YOU'RE 40. YOU GET MAIL FROM AARP WHEN YOU'RE 50. IN YOUR 60s, SOCIAL SECURITY...

JUDGING FROM THE CARD-STORE DISPLAY, YOU'RE OLD EVERY SINGLE BIRTHDAY!

SO WHEN DO YOU GET OLD?

I THINK IT'S WHEN RECESS GIVES WAY TO HAPPY HOUR.

DISTILLERS' MARKETING DEPARTMENTS CAUSE AGING?

DO YOU EVER WORRY ABOUT GETTING OLD?

HECK, NO! WE WORK AT AN ELEMENTARY SCHOOL!

I KNOW, I KNOW. THE KIDS KEEP US YOUNG...

NOT THAT SO MUCH.

YOU START OFF OLD AND GET IT OVER WITH.

EITHER OF YOU GEEZERS WANT TO SEE THIS ANTIQUE I FOUND?

I WONDER IF THERE'S ANYTHING MORE ROMANTIC THAN WALKING A DOG TOGETHER?

I DOUBT...

OH, SHOOT. I FORGOT TO GRAB A BAGGIE.

I BROUGHT BAGGIES.

BECAUSE I THINK WE'RE GOING TO NEED A BAGGIE.

I'VE GOT BAGGIES.

THANKS. I'M SORRY. WHERE WERE WE?

BETWEEN DELUSION AND DENIAL.